Animal, Vegetable, Mineral

Poems About Small Things

Animal,

Vegetable,

Mineral

Poems About Small Things

Selected by MYRA COHN LIVINGSTON

HarperCollins*Publishers*

Animal, Vegetable, Mineral
Poems About Small Things
Copyright © 1994 by Myra Cohn Livingston

Library of Congress Cataloging-in-Publication Data
Livingston, Myra Cohn
   Animal, vegetable, mineral : poems about small things / selected by
Myra Cohn Livingston.
       p.   cm.
   Summary: A collection of poems about some things that usually go unnoticed,
but are worth looking for, by authors such as Arnold Adoff, Karla Kuskin,
John Ciardi, and Charlotte Zolotow.
   ISBN 0-06-023008-8. — ISBN 0-06-023009-6 (lib. bdg.)
   1. Children's poetry.   [1. Poetry—Collections.]   I. Livingston, Myra Cohn.
PN6109.97.M66   1994   93-43712
808.81'0083—dc20   CIP
                                                                       AC

Typography by Carole Goodman
1   2   3   4   5   6   7   8   9   10
❖
First Edition

TABLE OF CONTENTS

ANIMAL

Animal

The chicken scratching
for food in the dirt stirs up
tiny tornados.

Kristine O'Connell George

LITTLE FISH

The tiny fish enjoy themselves
in the sea.
Quick little splinters of life,
their little lives are fun to them
in the sea.

D. H. Lawrence

SEA HORSE

Sea horse, sea horse,
come forward do,
make a big bow
to the people before you.
Sea horse, sea horse,
you can come out now,
the lady of the house
has sent for you.
Sea horse, sea horse,
you dance very well,
we might even call you
darling-sweet-boy.
Sea horse, sea horse,
it's time now, it's time,
to drift away slowly
go back to your place.

Folk song, Brazil

HEY, BUG!

Hey, bug, stay!
Don't run away.
I know a game that we can play.

I'll hold my fingers very still
and you can climb a finger-hill.

No, no.
Don't go.

Here's a wall—a tower, too,
a tiny bug town, just for you.
I've a cookie. You have some.
Take this oatmeal cookie crumb.

Hey, bug, stay!
Hey, bug!
Hey!

Lilian Moore

BEETLE

Shining Japanese beetle
eating the rose,
how your wings
glisten
like a small rainbow
in the sun!

Charlotte Zolotow

TO A FIREFLY

Flitting white-fire insect,
waving white-fire bug,
give me light before I go to sleep!
Come, little dancing white-fire bug,
come, little flitting white-fire beast,
light me with your bright white flame,
your little candle!

Chippewa

THE WASP

Where the ripe pears droop heavily
 The yellow wasp hums loud and long
 His hot and drowsy autumn song:
A yellow flame he seems to be,
 When darting suddenly from high
 He lights where fallen peaches lie:
Yellow and black, this tiny thing's
A tiger soul on elfin wings.

       William Sharp

DRAGONFLY

In the land of evening, blue dragonfly
is skimming over the water.
Only his tail touches,
as his wings flap and rustle.

Pima

THE SNAIL

Little snail,
Dreaming you go.
Weather and rose
Is all you know.

Weather and rose
Is all you see,
Drinking the dewdrop's
Mystery.

Langston Hughes

THE PRAYER OF THE
GLOW-WORM

Dear God,
would You take Your light
a little farther away
from me?
I am like a morsel
of cinder
and need Your night
for my heart to dare
to flicker out its feeble star:
its hope, to give to other hearts,
what can be stolen from all poverty—
a gleam of joy.

Amen.

Carmen Bernos de Gasztold
(translated by Rumer Godden)

COCOON

The little caterpillar creeps
Awhile before in silk it sleeps.
It sleeps awhile before it flies,
And flies awhile before it dies,
And that's the end of three good tries.

David McCord

THE VIRUS

A Virus crouched upon the terrace
Watching for someone he might harass,
Then hurled himself with malice fierce
Upon a human, name of Pierce;
While Albert Pierce could but respond, "Hey,
Shoo!" and had him till next Monday.

Christian Morgenstern
(translated by Lore Segal and W. D. Snodgrass)

NIGHT DANCERS

Their quick feet pattered on the grass
    As light as dewdrops fall.
I saw their shadows on the glass
    And heard their voices call.

But when I went out hurrying
    To join them, they were gone.
I only found a little ring
    Of footprints on the lawn.

Thomas Kennedy

Where the bee sucks, there suck I:
    In a cowslip's bell I lie;
There I couch when owls do cry.
On the bat's back I do fly
After summer merrily:
    Merrily, merrily shall I live now
    Under the blossom that hangs on the bough.

William Shakespeare

EGG

Reader, in your hand you hold
A silver case, a box of gold.
I have no door, however small,
Unless you pierce my tender wall,
And there's no skill in healing then
Shall ever make me whole again.
Show pity, Reader, for my plight:
Let be, or else consume me quite.

Jay MacPherson

BUTTERFLY SONG

Butterfly, butterfly, butterfly, butterfly,
Oh, look, see it hovering among the flowers,
It is like a baby trying to walk and not knowing how to go.
The clouds sprinkle down the rain.

Acoma

EARTHWORMS

Garden soil,
Spaded up,
Gleams with
Gravel-glints,
Mica-sparks, and
Bright wet
Glimpses of
Earthworms
Stirring beneath:

Put on the palm,
Still rough
With crumbs,
They roll and
Glisten in the sun
As fresh
As new rubies
Dug out of
Deepest earth.

Valerie Worth

Vegetable

THE FAIRY RING

Here the horse-mushrooms make a fairy ring,
  Some standing upright and some overthrown,
A small Stonehenge, where heavy black slugs cling
  And bite away, like Time, the tender stone.

Andrew Young

MISTLETOE

Mistletoe new,
Mistletoe old,
Cut it down
With a knife of gold.

Mistletoe green,
Mistletoe milk,
Let it fall
On a scarf of silk.

Mistletoe from
The Christmas oak,
Keep my house
From lightning stroke.

Guard from thunder
My roof-tree
And any evil
That there be.

Charles Causley

DANCE OF THE MUSHROOMS

Mushrooms tipping their caps—
    this is all you ever see.

        But when night falls
           through the trees,
      and no one is watching,
            they brown shyly
           and begin to dance.

             Bowing softly,
        they waltz in the dark
        to the wind's guitar.
        But when light falls
        through the trees,

mushrooms tipping their caps—
    this is all you ever see.

J. Patrick Lewis

JACARANDA BLUE

All over town, blue
clouds have touched down on branches—
without being punctured?

No, look—they're leaking
one blossom at a time *(splash)*
in each blue puddle.

John Ridland

Getting The Sweet

                              strawberries
from my
fingers
        down
        into the basket
without
        eating all of them
                              up
                              is
        the problem

        the solution
                      is
                  not
          to solve
          the problem
until
      you
        are
      full
          of answers

                    Arnold Adoff

RADISH

The radish is
the only dish
that isn't flat
but spherical.

Eating small
green peas off it
could make you quite
hysterical.

N. M. Bodecker

THISTLES

Thirty thirsty thistles
Thicketed and green
Growing in a grassy swamp
Purple-topped and lean
Prickly and thistly
Topped by tufts of thorns
Green mean little leaves on them
And tiny purple horns
Briary and brambly
A spiky, spiney bunch of them.
A troop of bright-red birds came by
And had a lovely lunch of them.

Karla Kuskin

SWEET PEAS

Here are sweet peas, on tiptoe for a flight,
With wings of gentle flush o'er delicate white,
And taper fingers catching at all things,
To bind them all about with tiny rings.

John Keats

BLUEBELLS AND FOXGLOVES

If bluebells could be rung
   In early summer time,
The sound you'd hear would be
   A small, silvery chime.

The bells on foxglove spires,
   If they could once be tolled,
Would give a mellow sound
   As deep and rich as gold.

The bluebells and foxgloves—
   If they together pealed,
Who knows what elfin footsteps
   Would crowd across the field?

James Reeves

THE LEAVES ARE GREEN

The leaves are green, the nuts are brown,
They hang so high they won't come down.
Leave them alone till frosty weather,
Then they will all come down together.

Old rhyme

JOURNEY

I slid into the stem of the chrysanthemum
and lay back on the leaf of the lily
I swung myself across the trumpet vine
and climbed among the petals of the peas
and last I skimmed the spikes of grass
wearing my sandals to avoid the thrust of gorse
and when I came to rest under the screening of the violets
I was what I had wished
stained green, a part of them.

Julia Cunningham

THINGS AS THEY ARE

Beetles that blow in the breeze
on stems—may be berries.

Marbles that grow on trees—
mostly are cherries.

Norma Farber

TREES: THE SEEDS

We are
given light wings,
parachutes, downy legs
that we may be carried aloft
by wind

and drop
where some kind mouse
will bury us in earth;
some squirrel will forget we are food,
leave us

to sprout
green shoots, to weave
rootlets, that we may eat
and drink and grow in time our own
small seeds

Myra Cohn Livingston

INVITATION STANDING

Bring a leaf to me
just a leaf just a
spring leaf, an
april leaf
just
     come

Blue sky
never mind
Spring rain
never mind
Reach up and
take a leaf and
     come
just come

Paul Blackburn

from SONGS IN THE GARDEN OF THE HOUSE GOD

1.

The sacred blue corn-seed I am planting,
In one night it will grow and flourish,
In one night the corn increases,
In the garden of the House God.

The sacred white corn-seed I am planting,
In one day it will grow and ripen,
In one day the corn increases,
In its beauty it increases.

Navaho

SEEDS

The seeds I sowed—
For week unseen—
Have pushed up pygmy
Shoots of green;
So frail you'd think
The tiniest stone
Would never let
A glimpse be shown.

But no; a pebble
Near them lies,
At least a cherry-stone
In size,
Which that mere sprout
Has heaved away,
To bask in sunshine,
See the Day.

Walter de la Mare

ORIENTAL POPPY

Petal of a poppy
(Though one could have said
Butterfly wing)
Orange origami
Shaped in crepe paper
By a Japanese.

Felice Holman

MILKWEED

In the soft summer air
a piece of fluff from some milkweed
drifts by
like a little floating cloud
full of seeds

Charlotte Zolotow

Mineral

AN AMULET

A-
round
my neck
an amu-
let
Be-
tween
my eyes
a star
A
ring
in my
nose
and a
gold
chain
to
Keep me
where
you
are

Samuel Menashe

A CHINESE TOY

Six whittled chickens
on a wooden bat

that peck within a
circle pulled

by strings fast to
a hanging weight

when shuttled by the
playful hand

William Carlos Williams

MOTE

Dust-speck in a sunbeam,
I blow a breath, you soar,
Revolving like some mighty moon
For spacefolk to explore.

What will you show them? Roads of gold
Where chariots and dragons race?
A princess dressed in spidery silk
With moonlight all over her face?

Your people—do they raise tall trees
Or trash heaps? Build or wreck?
Play ball, or play at war to win
The right to rule you, speck?

When, tired of circling in the sun,
You care to spend tonight,
Drift down. Take my fingertip
For your landing site.

X. J. Kennedy

SETTLING INTO A NEW HOUSE

little things
turn up at last
as you put the house
back together—
the nozzle
for the sink tap,
the nightlight—
small bits of a
slow puzzle

John Ridland

MY TOOTH

Beneath
my pillow,
buried deep
like treasure,
from the dark it speaks
of ivory crumbled
with sharp stone,
of crystal ground
with tooth and bone,
of marble crushed
with pearl: when mixed
and sifted down
will shine, and with
one quick pinch
of powdered tusk,
makes magic—
makes the fairies' dust.

Deborah Chandra

KNOTHOLES

To make a knothole,
Knock out the knot;
And having a knothole,
What have you got?
You've got whatever
The fence shut in.
With lots of knots,
Where they have been
You've got whatever
The fence shut out.
You see what knotholes
Are all about?

David McCord

HOW TO ASSEMBLE A TOY

This is the whatsit that fits on the knob
Of the gadget that turns the thingamabob.
This is the dingus that fits in place
With the doodad next to the whosiface.
This is the jigger that goes in the hole
Where the gizmo turns the rigamarole.
Now slip the ding-dang into the slot
Of the jugamalug, and what have you got?

It's a genuine neverwas such a not!

John Ciardi

A SINGLE PENNY

A single penny
does not jingle
in my pocket,
but two would
make a single
jingle
and would do.
And three
would be
a real
tympani!

Felice Holman

TIME PIECE

Take the back off the watch
and see that universe of small parts,
bobbing and turning,
each doing what it should be doing,
and ignoring you completely.

William Cole

SONG OF THE MARBLE EARRINGS

We might have been hall or wall of a stately palace
Or an altarpiece looking down on a silver chalice,
Or a table top in the best hotel in Dallas,
But who wouldn't rather (bearing Texas no malice)
Sit in the lovely lobe of the ear of Alice?

Lillian Morrison

I need not your needles, they're needless to me;
For kneading of needles were needless, you see;
But did my neat trousers but need to be kneed,
I then should have need of your needles indeed.

Nursery rhyme

A little child
Picked with his fingers
A drop of dew—
And lo, it vanished!

Issa
(translated by Nobuyuki Yuasa)

SNOW STARS

Once there was a girl
who spoke diamonds
when she opened
her mouth
to say hello.

I breathe my
hello
against the freezing
glass
and diamonds blow
out of my mouth.
They prism the pane
with landscapes etched
in silver.

Once there was a girl
whose breath
filled a winter day
with stars.

Barbara Juster Esbensen

PEBBLES

Pebbles belong to no one
Until you pick them up—
Then they are yours.

But which, of all the world's
Mountains of little broken stones,
Will you choose to keep?

The smooth black, the white,
The rough gray with sparks
Shining in its cracks?

Somewhere the best pebble must
Lie hidden, meant for you
If you can find it.

Valerie Worth

WHO WOULD MARRY
A MINERAL?

Who would marry a mineral
No matter how precious,
Out of geologic time,
Shining by refraction;

Molded by long process,
Moved by light, not love,
Quartz, a geode, the eye of a cat
Who would marry that?

Lillian Morrison

INDEX OF AUTHORS AND TRANSLATORS

INDEX OF FIRST LINES

The radish is, *28*
The sacred blue corn-seed
    I am planting, *37*
The seeds I sowed—, *38*
The tiny fish enjoy them-
    selves, *4*
Their quick feet pattered
    on the grass, *15*
Thirty thirsty thistles, *29*
This is the whatsit that
    fits on the knob, *49*

To make a knothole, *48*
We are, *35*
We might have been hall
    or wall of a stately
    palace, *52*
Where the bee sucks,
    there suck I:, *16*
Where the ripe pears
    droop heavily, *9*
Who would marry a
    mineral?, *57*

INDEX OF TITLES

ACKNOWLEDGMENTS

Every effort has been made to trace the ownership of all copyrighted material and to secure the necessary permissions to reprint these selections. In the event of any question arising as to the use of any material, the editor and the publisher, while expressing regret for any inadvertent error, will be happy to make the necessary correction in future printings. Thanks are due to the following for permission to reprint the copyrighted materials listed below:

A. R. Beal, for "Bluebells and Foxgloves" by James Reeves, from *The Blackbird in the Lilac*.

Mrs. Paul Blackburn, for "Invitation Standing" by Paul Blackburn, from *The Cities*, 1969.

William Cole, for "Time Piece" by William Cole. Copyright © by William Cole. Used by permission of the author.

Julia Cunningham, for "Journey" by Julia Cunningham. Used by permission of the author. Copyright © by Julia Cunningham 1994.

Thomas Farber, for "Things as They Are" from *Small Wonders* by Norma Farber, published by Coward, McCann & Geoghegan, Inc. Copyright © by Thomas Farber.

Farrar, Straus & Giroux, Inc., for "Butterfly Song" and part one from "Songs in the Garden of the House God" from *In the Trail of the Wind* edited by John Bierhorst. Copyright © 1971 by John Bierhorst. "My Tooth" from *Rich Lizard* by Deborah Chandra. Copyright © 1993 by Deborah Chandra. "Earthworms" from *More Small Poems* by Valerie Worth. Copyright © 1976 by Valerie Worth. "Pebbles" from *Small Poems* by Valerie Worth. Copyright © 1972 by Valerie Worth. All reprinted by permission of Farrar, Straus & Giroux, Inc.